Rainbows in my eyes

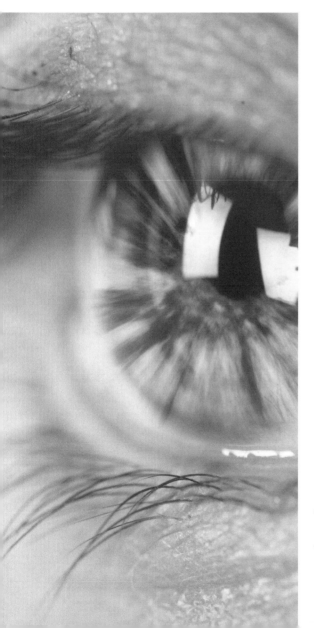

A collection of poems by

J.K. Rowbory

First published in 2009
Second impression 2010

Text copyright © Jennifer Karen Rowbory 2009

The author Jennifer Karen Rowbory asserts the right to be
identified as the author of this work.

ISBN 978-1-4082-4968-0

Printed and bound in Great Britain by Ashford Colour Press

Front cover photo by Shutterstock/Macs Peter
Front flap photo by Ann Rowbory
Biography page photo by Hannah Kamen
Contents page photo by Shutterstock/Bruce Amos

Biography

Jenny Rowbory was born in 1986 in Ashford,
Middlesex, and currently lives in Ashbocking,
Suffolk. During her first year at university in 2004,
she became ill with a virus that caused severe
Myalgic Encephalomyelitis (M.E.) (inflammation
of the brain and spinal cord). M.E. affects all
bodily systems, causing Jenny to be bed-bound
and unable to sit up because of strain on her
cardiovascular system. Her poems mean a lot to
her and she hopes that other people may resonate
with some of them or find meaning in them too.

The money made from the sale of this anthology
will go towards her medical costs.

Contents

My day

I waltz through the clouds
catching white wisps in my hair
and glide over the oceans
trailing my finger on the surface
leaving miles of ripples in my wake.
I breaststroke through the air
over cities, towns, villages,
empty deserts and emerald jungle swathes.
I zoom across the world
letting myself go limp when
swept up in violent hurricanes
and am flung crazily around tornados.
I ride on the peaks of freak waves
in the-middle-of-nowhere-sea
and pulse along in rhythm with swarms
of electric blue and rose Beroe jellyfish,
otherworldly and stark against the black depths
of the Marianas Trench.
I do a jig on the summit of Everest
and blast out of an erupting volcano
just millimetres ahead of the pyroclastic death
and am slammed up, up through the atmosphere,
orbiting the Earth.

Heartcry

Surely the very fabric of the universe
must be bending, must be vibrating.
Surely my pain must be felt
in the houses down the street,
down the town,
down the county.
Violent shockwaves pulse out from my epicentre,
such is the intensity of my grief.
Surely something must happen,
surely there must be a response to my agony.
But my room stares back at me in silence.
Invisibly, silently,
God's arms wrap around me so closely
that the sobs that wrack my body
convulse him too.

Can't you be a magician, God?

Can't you be a magician, God,
if only for one day?
Forget about being wise and good
and do exactly what I say.

Can't our prayers be spells, God,
if only for one day?
The right words in the right order
and bingo! we'll have our way.

Make me better *now*, Lord,
please no more delay.
I want to force your hand, Lord,
to make my illness go away.

Held

Pinned here
I kick and scream,
try to punch my way out.
But your arms are too strong.

Pinned here
I sulk and ignore you,
try to freeze you out.
But you are too patient.

Pinned here
I spit and abuse you,
try to provoke you.
But your love is too great.

Pinned here
I cry,
break your heart with my pain.
But you will not let go.

Pinned here,
too exhausted to wrestle any more.
In the stillness I see
I'm in an embrace not a headlock.

The rainbow bird

Once there was a bird
the size of an ostrich
but with feathers of glass
that ruffled in the wind
as any feather would.
It was an unearthly glass,
weightless and delicate.

In the sun
rays hit its plumage
as if the feathers were prisms,
and scattered
fantastically chaotically
in all directions
in awkward impossible angles
so that rainbows were everywhere,
absolutely everywhere.

In the sun
this bird was a
shimmering ocean –
glorious in its simple splendour.
It travelled the earth
bringing light and rainbows,
rainbows and light,
hope for the rag-tag bunch
of animals
who followed it
wherever it went.
Squirrels, rats, weasels, snakes
and animals of every kind
followed in its wake,
just desperate to be
in its presence, with its light.
Eagles circled above,
dolphins raced along the coast
when it walked by the sea,
just for a single glimpse
of its beauty.

But one awful day
it was snatched away
by greedy men
who wanted its glass feathers
for their own.

Our bird was taken
to the deepest darkest
place that ever there was,
where the very air
was thick with evil
and horror.
It was flung
into the blackest of black pits
and began to be excruciatingly
plucked of every last feather.

But something happened
that the evil men did not expect.
The very moment
that each feather was yanked
off its back,
the feathers changed.
They hardened,
became too heavy to even hold,
and so fell,
shattered on the stony ground,
just broken shards of glass.

These remnants were, of course,
useless to the men,
so they tortured our bird,
lashed it raw and close to death.
They left it alone for months
in the solitary pit
to see if any more feathers
would grow... but none did.
So they beat it more
until it was struggling for breath
and left it for dead.

For months and years
it hung on in the complete darkness,
shrivelled and scarred,
surviving second by second
minute by minute.

Just by chance
in a storm,
a tree was brought crashing
into our bird's pit.
Weak and limp
it tried and failed
over and over again
to haul itself up and out
until victory!
It was free...
free as a naked,
unfeathered, shrunken
shadow of itself.
It limped the way back
along its old haunts.
But the eagles
didn't even notice
and the dolphins swam past
without a second glance.
Our bird passed foxes, beetles,
stoats, mice, deer and
every sort of creature.
None of them
recognised it.
Some even mocked
its pathetic form
as it hobbled by.

Our bird stopped
and rested in a glade
for a while.
A butterfly landed on its beak.
'It's you! The rainbow bird!'
the butterfly squeaked.
Surprised, our bird rasped
'How did you know?'

The butterfly replied
'Because you have rainbows
in your eyes.
But how can this be?
Your glass feathers
are gone so where
are the rainbows
coming from?'
The butterfly was confused.

Our bird laughed wheezily
and explained,
'The light that shone
on the glass feathers
to make the rainbows
never did come from the sun.
Some days it was sunny,
others not,
but light still bounced off
my feathers,
there were always rainbows.
No, the light came
from inside me;
I am the light.

'They stole my feathers,
broke my body,
took my friends.
But my light cannot die.
It kept me alive
in complete darkness.
Even in the pit
when no-one could see,
I still had rainbows in my eyes
from the light prisms
inside me.'

The butterfly paused.
'But you're unsightly
and scarred and old now.
Who will want to follow you
around or be your friend?
Not everyone can see

your eyes like I can,
perched here on your beak.
How will they know
you're you?
How will they see
the rainbows
in your eyes?'
the butterfly asked.

'I guess,' our bird answered,
'they'll just have to
take a closer look,
get to know me again.'

The butterfly was fretting now.
'But who's going to do that?
The dolphins are busy swimming,
the eagles are busy hunting,
in fact, everyone is always busy,
too busy to take a closer look.
What are you going to do?
What are you going to do?'

'Dear, precious butterfly,
they will come to know
me if they want to.
The light is in me and
they can have it for themselves
if they ask me.
And you can have it too, butterfly.'

Our bird breathed on the butterfly
and it glowed with light.
'See now, you have rainbows
in your eyes too, butterfly.'

The excited butterfly zipped
and loop-the-looped in delight.

'Will you tell them for me, butterfly?
Tell them my story,
that the rainbows
and light

that they were so hungry
to see and follow before,
they can have for themselves.
Before, they could only see
my beauty,
now they can *have* it
inside them.

'Then they can have
my light presence within
and we can always
be together.
They can follow me
wherever they are in the world
because I'll be with them inside.
I'll be swimming along with the dolphins
and soaring with the eagles,
sharing their pleasure,
sharing their lives,
spirit to Spirit,
light to Light.'

So the elated butterfly flew
away to tell the others.
Not everyone
believed it
or would listen.
But as the butterfly
often said to them,
'Who *wouldn't* want
rainbows in their eyes
and light in their hearts?'

Let me in

You've all twizzled layers
of bubblewrap around yourselves,
always unpopped,
a barrier you never let me past.
Only a blurred version of you
can be seen from outside,
a vague figure through frosted glass.
You never let me see.
You never let me see.

He is not here

I want to go in and
smash the stained-glass windows,
chop the altar in two,
squeeze spurts of tomato ketchup
onto the walls and
stamp jam into the carpets.
I want to go in and
get some chainsaw action going
on the hard cold pews and
flamethrow the hanging banners,
chuck several cans of bright pink paint
over the heavy oak doors,
yank the clangers from their bells,
rip up the children's pictures
on the Sunday School display and
hurl after-service mugs and teacups
to shatter against the font.
He is not here.
We are his home now,
not bricks and mortar.
The rampage of Jesus' death
tore the separating curtain apart.

Invasion

I.

A butterfly lazily floats over a hedge.

Early-morning crisp silence,
endless-possibilities mist,
wind still asleep.
The muddy track carves around the perimeter
of the dewy, Granny Smith field
into the forest;
rows of ancient dignitaries line the way
to the king, who stands tall
and proud,
contentedly surveying his kingdom.
Soggy slices of bark mix
in a mosaic with
the banana, chocolate and strawberry
carpet of leaves
skirting the path.
Seedlings compete to grow as big as their grandfathers,
stretching their hands upwards
towards the light filtering through
the canopy overhead,
doodling ditzily on the dull earth.
A mystery world,
buzzing inaudibly but tangibly
with the magic pulsing through it,
hinting at something you once knew.
You can hear the forest breathe.

II.

Shouts and noise fill the field,
the morning rudely awoken.
Families with laid-down rugs are
strewn across the dry patchy grass;
children play games
bulldozing painstakingly-spun webs.
Into the wood,
the once-king stands ashamed
and vulnerable,
heart-shaped carvings tattooing his skin.
The grandfathers grieve their crushed grandchildren,
no longer reaching up
to the large clumps of light
falling through the thin canopy;
many trees were martyred,
now part of a park bench somewhere.
Emerging back into the open,
the stench
of public toilets
and fly-engulfed bins
blasts the nostrils.
Graffitied walls boast of their colours,
a taunt to the distressed trees,
their quiet magic leached away.
You can hear the forest wheezing.

A butterfly hurriedly streaks over a hedge.

Dayspring

Strange
how suddenly a moment of clarity
can whiplash into this unreality,
how out of the depths of deep
a switch turns on,
the circuit complete –
a surge of dazzling consciousness,
a stunning shock of truth,
slamming you into the electric present –
no longer more asleep than awake,
finally out of auto-coma.

Mummy

Jesus was silent
but you spoke to me.
Jesus was absent
but you were there.
Jesus' hands were still
but yours rubbed my feet.
Jesus' arms were full
but yours hugged me.
Thank you
for being Jesus to me –
his heart, hands and feet.
You keep me going;
I think I would break
without you.

The never-ending storm

Megaclouds in a murderous black roil,
a relentless bombardment of machine-gun rain,
waves in a violent washing-machine churn,
Superman-breath winds with
a jellyfish-stingered whip.
Years of continuous barrage
and yet it still rages.
This is it.
It has come.
The never-ending storm.

This is the perpetual storm,
no break, no respite.
No-one here has any power
to stop it.
The One over there though
can end it,
but is not doing so
at present.
Just the teasing dangled hope
of the donkey's always just-out-of-reach carrot.

How much longer
will it batter?
How much longer?

A fleeting visit

My fixed portion of the world,
my rectangular allocation of life:
my window.
There are never any birds
in the tops of the
two sole trees
that, along with the sky,
completely fill the picture
on my four-cornered screen,
but today
first there was one
and then another.
Two birds.
So tiny and fragile
but then gone
in a heartbeat,
snatched away.
But still,
a special gift
just for me
today,
my two little visitors.

Honoured

Eric Liddell
ran for Go(l)d in the Olympics
and then in China,
held firm to his integrity;
his life honoured God.
You can read about it in a book
or watch it in a film.

William Wilberforce
persevered in his campaign,
helped bring a beginning to an end of slavery,
overcoming injustice;
his life honoured God.
You can read about it in a book
or watch it in a film.

Gladys Aylward
showed God's love through her love for others,
brave amidst great danger,
patiently persisted over a lifetime;
her life honoured God.
You can read about it in a book
or watch it in a film.

Corrie ten Boom
courageously sheltered those in peril,
suffered greatly for it in a concentration camp,
yet was full of love, forgiveness and joy;
her life honoured God.
You can read about it in a book
or watch it in a film.

Someone lies in great agony forever on a bed,
thoughts are a physical activity for one who can barely move,
one who has always to bear to receive help, never give it,
who loves God, but often slides away to escape reality and pain,
but always comes back, just about.
This nothingness would make poor reading,
one and a half hours of this would make poor viewing.

'Faith without works is dead.'
Can faith become a work itself,
thought equal an action?
Only God notices the deedless form on the bed
(who no-one will see, hear or read about)
and bends close and strokes their brow.
An unspoken bond; each living breath an honour to him.

What now?

What now, child of light?
What now,
now your tongue has been whet with darkness?
You cannot scratch off the scales from your eyes
or gouge out the memories from your mind.
Oh broken heart:
look!
Where once there was one heart,
since the whole has been riven apart,
it has become two.
And when the bleeding from the split
finally abates and heals over,
you'll be carrying two whole hearts,
aching with twice the pain
but also with twice the hope,
twice the love.

Lost in translation

Even the richest language is in poverty
with regard to our purpose,
so we mind-rifle for the best-matched word
in conceded shared human language,
unsatisfyingly inaccurate and restricting for
our own personal soul-tongue,
unique to each individual,
unlimited and untameable by alphabet and grammar,
both amorphous and distinct, unbearably potent:
words are a size too small.
Yet, the emotion aches to be expressed,
unceasingly banging against our inner walls,
trying to break free;
so, we write –
the coloured inks of our hearts
leaching out through pen,
not fully fulfilled
through the black ink of the page.

Alive

Though unable to move
every exhalation from my nostrils is a song,
through all the agony
each painful heartbeat is an exultant drum,
each thump of my hurting head
a crash of triumphant cymbals,
each whirl of dizziness
a dance of spinning twirls;
my body is weak, yet,
to be alive is praise.

Crux

Tentatively toe-testing the waters
of the Rubicon,
nervously glancing around,
longing to linger on these safe, gentle banks;
dare you cross?

Twines of racing thought knot themselves
round your brain but
nothing ventured nothing gained so,
with a sharp intake of breath,
eyes tight shut, you place
that first irrevocable step.

Eyelids lifting
your feet plant one wet step after another,
waging war with your mind,
blocking its miasmous doubts
but letting your heart filter in –
allowing Hope and Possibility to lead you by the hand
and carry you trembling through.

Christmas

You are my treasure,
my pearl beyond price.
I forsake all my riches,
my wealth in heaven,
to come and seek you out.

Pedestal

Am I a fool
that my mind should gush
about how delicious it is to be well?
To linger on thoughts of running and jumping about,
turning them round in my mouth with my tongue
like savouring my favourite dish?
As I am, ill,
up on a pedestal is
the freedom to be able to move, even breathe,
without a thought to
the immense effort and strength
needed to do so;
up on a pedestal is
the energy to be able to have emotion –
to laugh or to cry,
to be who you are
without the balaclava of illness
stifling it.

So, would I be a fool
when I become well,
to have a can't-help-myself grin
splashed across my face
at the wonder of every step?
Will the sandpaper of time on the memory and
the eroding waves of the commonplace replacing novelty
eat away at the base of that pedestal and
bring it crashing down?

Sleep pod

Every night
in my head I go
into my sleep pod:
a snugly-fitting
human-sized
luxurious cuboid,
thickly padded
on every inside facet
with heavenly bedding,
clean, white and soft.
Here it is the end of time,
here it is silent.
Everything is over,
everything is completed,
finished, made right.
Nothing exists outside the pod,
nothing and no-one can get to me.
I am safe,
everyone I know is safe.
I've done my time
and I did gooood.
Now it's my turn,
my time to relax;
there is nothing more
to do or think.
Now I can sleep.

So I wait

You are always enough, they say.
Why then am I left so empty?
So let down, so disappointed.
Is there something so wrong with me,
so abhorrent,
that you would leave me an orphan
but parent everyone else?
I cannot see you
or hear you
or feel you.
I cry out for strength to cope
but you leave me even weaker
than I was to begin with
when you fail to give it.
You promised to give it,
you gave your Word.
What on earth am I meant to think?

And yet I believe.
I cannot help it –
I know it's the truth,
you're the truth.
And I still love,
I love so very deeply.
That's why all this hurts so much.

Therefore I will wait,
though feeling abandoned,
confused,
seriously wounded.
I am bleeding to death, Lord.
Come quickly.

Quest for the holy grail

Through desert storms, mountain blizzards,
over canyons on a one-foot wide bridge,
through entanglements of jungle vines,
I desperately trudged.

You see, my health had been
kidnapped, taken –
nobody knew precisely where,
and I certainly had no clue.

Determined, I marched on,
through countless mires and bogs,
until I arrived at a village in a clearing,
mud huts and all!

Guards swarmed everywhere.
This was it – I had arrived;
this must be where
my health was being held hostage.

After all my travels,
it was all confounded
when I accidentally fell over a log –
my position to the guards made plain.

As I was led to the largest hut,
two guards gripping each arm,
I was taken by surprise
at what I found inside.

A deceivingly civil scene met my eyes:
my health was in a chair, not bound,
opposite a desk
at which a man was seated –
a smiling man in a suit.
'How can I help you?'
he asked cheerily.

For a few moments silence reigned
as I adjusted to the surreal scene.
'I just want my health back,'
I replied, braver than I felt.

Softly spoken, the man began,
'*You* see your health
sitting in the chair before me.
Apparently you do not have it
and have been searching for it
exhaustively.
But I have been taught
by my educators
that it is not there.
So, I do not see anything
sitting in this chair before me.
To me, the chair is empty.
There is no reason to search
for your health here
or investigate it any further.
I will not help you
in your quest.'

In desperation I spluttered
'But it's there! Just there!
I can see it! Let me have it!
What use is it to you?'

The man smiled,
'Oh it's of no use to me.
I just don't believe I *have* it
so I don't have the power
to free it
because it's not there.'

Suddenly I was no longer in the hut,
no longer in the clearing,
no longer even in the jungle.
I was lying in my bed at home
and an NHS doctor was speaking.

Internal fireworks

All of a jitter, all of a dither,
standing then sitting
standing then sitting
and bouncing up once more;
insides itching
fingers twitching
heart fidgeting,
pacing up and down,
down and up,
spontaneously grinning,
bubbles of anticipation racing
each other
up my throat from my chest –
too much excitement to hold
in just one body!

Lost

How did I manage to lose my way,
lose my way in these woods?
The directions were simple,
the path clear,
so how on earth did I end up *here*?
Here,
where *is* that exactly?
Here,
where the trees are so close
and the dark fogs my eyes.

Oh that some great winged creature were to come
and lift me up with powerful talons,
raising my head above these tall, tall trees
so I could see my way home.

But alas it is not to be so
and I do not know where I am going –
whether I wander further and further into this prison
of twisting, entangling branches
or whether I get closer to home.
Retracing my steps is impossible;
I have come so very far.

Oh that I had not wandered from the route,
the route given to me by my Friend;
but my way had seemed so much more alluring –
my path was lined with crispy leaves
ready to crunch underfoot,
the foliage rustling with the promise
of little animals to be glimpsed;
at first it had gone so well
but all I have got is lost.

Scrambled

A child's violent black scribble:
a dark buzzing mass of tangled lines,
persistent and definite in its existence,
staring out at you, defiant, brazen,
uncompromisingly there.
This hub of confusion and knots,
mercilessly spiralling, entangling, merging,
this mass oscillates perpetually,
a high-pitched unrelenting hum
suspended in my head.

Blur

Waiting, waiting,
just riding out the days,
waiting for them to pass
one
after another
and then
the next
and the day after,
over and over,
infinitely
lolling by
merging together,
watching the months simultaneously fly
and crawl.
During it
each hour lasts a year,
looking back
each year lasts an hour.

This battlefield

This battlefield
is not an obvious one.
Unaware of the fight raging,
unarmoured and unarmed,
you're unprotected from harm.
This enemy's arrows
are invisible,
subtle in approach,
but you have no shield
to defend yourself from attack –
you don't even know you're *being* attacked!
No physical wounds appear,
no gashes or bleeding flesh;
no, these assaults penetrate
much, much deeper,
destroy something
much, much dearer.

Night-time

What power is it that startles me awake
at night's deepest black,
summoning me to panic and a frenzied heart?
What invisible force holds me down,
pinning fright-stiff limbs to the bed?
Ears of mine, why do you strain
to hear unimaginable terrors
through the dread writhing silence,
prickling with evil?
Air, how do you move when there is no breeze
and come to chill my skin with fear?
You horror of darkness that prowls my nights,
I shall conquer you with Light!

I want you back

Why are you hiding?
What made you run?
I see you,
you who are crouched in that squalid corner,
exhausted, scared, covered in dirt,
bewildered and confused at exactly how you got there.
All misery and shame are yours.
You think there's no way back
but *I am* the way –
I'm the one who *makes* the ways!
And I will make a way back just for you.
I will work night and day to clear the paths
and not stop 'til it is finished,
then I will come and crouch next to you in your corner,
point to the path I have made,
lift you in my strong arms
and carry you, drained and filthy as you are,
carry you all the way back home.

The librarian

Rows of bottles
filled with my tears
line shelf after shelf
in a library of my pain.
Not a single teardrop
is missing:
you've caught every one.
Man of sorrows,
lovingly stacking
the shelves,
each drop is recorded,
written in your book.
You don't forget,
don't neglect
even one.

Stuck in the mud

I'm good at this game, I am,
I'm the fastest and the slipperiest,
impossibly twisting and turning
away from our pursuer,
never getting caught.
Look at *me*! Look at me go!
Here and there I speed and duck,
crawling through pairs of frozen legs
to unstick them, set them free;
they can always count on *me*!
…
It was one risk too many I guess,
thought I could crawl through in time
before the hovering pursuer closed in,
even if it was a trap (which it was)
because I was the best.
Should have known better.
So here I am,
standing alone, abandoned by the others
since now it's raining hard
and dark storm clouds boil overhead,
with arms out and legs apart, stuck fast,
stuck in the mud.
Who will come?

Release

Chains might have bound her hands and feet
and bars blocked the windows
for all the difference it would have made:
illness was her crime.

From the miry bottom of the bog
the first shoot of a lotus flower stirred and reached out
upwards, upwards, through the murky waters,
ever straining towards the light.

Time might have been fast-forwarded
and years have been skipped
for all the difference it would have made:
illness was her sentence.

Surfacing into the dark shadows of thick jungle,
the shoot burst forth, floundering for a moment
before thirstily drinking in the faintest ray of light;
a bud began to form.

Summer might have been winter
and warmth replaced with cold
for all the difference it would have made:
illness was her bolted dungeon door to the outside world.

Blooming gradually into glowing white, soft petals,
it was dwarfed by the impenetrable matt of vines, ooze and gloom,
invisible and unknown to the world, deep in untouched rainforest;
but no difference did it make:

for it was in the dark *bottom of the bog*
that she had become thirsty for the light –
sought it, *strained for it,* found it, *bathed in it*:
illness was her *seed of* freedom.

Time to say goodbye

It is long overdue.
I should force my love
to say goodbye to you.
But my love wants to cling,
it wants to keep its beat.

So it is stranded,
a beached whale
alone on the empty shore.
Its ancient eyes can see the end
but it hangs on yet.

It has no idea
how to die
after surviving
against all reason
for so long.

It is long overdue.
I should force my love
to say goodbye to you.
But my love wants to cling,
it wants to keep its beat.